# A Giant in High Heels

Mary Claire Brink Watts
Illustrated by Ishmam Ahmed

Windigo Press
Plymouth, Minnesota

Text copyright © 2021 Mary Watts

Illustration copyright © 2021 Ishmam Ahmed

Published by Windigo Press, Plymouth, Minnesota

All rights reserved.

No part of this publication may be reproduced, transmitted, or sold without written permission.

For permission or purchasing inquiries, please contact marywatts@q.com.

Library of Congress Control Number: 2021908324

ISBN: 978-0-578-95944-3

For Dolores, Nina, Ben, and Marion

In one graceful move, Twizzle hopped into the shallow water and dragged her canoe ashore. She'd lost her favorite fishing lure but had caught a fine fat trout.

The tall pines reached out, welcoming her home. The waves clapped against the shoreline, celebrating her catch.

Twizzle's mouth watered as the fish sizzled over the fire. She wished she had a friend to share her meal.

Twizzle ran to the garden for some onions to throw in the skillet. But where was the gate? And what happened to all her vegetables?

"I like veggie burgers but not veggie burglars." Twizzle chuckled nervously, trying to comfort herself.

In the trampled mess that used to be her garden, she spotted a clue—huge footprints with spike marks in the back, like a giant in high heels. She followed the tracks until they disappeared on the forest floor.

After lunch, Twizzle headed to the backyard to grab her clothes from the line where they were drying in the morning sun. But her clothes and clothesline were gone.

"A gust of wind must have blown them away."

Twizzle looked around for her clothes. That's when she saw the footprints again—the giant in high heels.

She followed the footprints past the trees where her hammock hung. But her hammock was nowhere to be seen.

Twizzle picked up a large branch in case she needed to defend herself against the giant in high heels.

A loud crash startled Twizzle. It couldn't be thunder. There was only one wispy cloud in the sky, like a hint of white paint on a blue canvas.

"It was too loud to be a beaver slapping its tail on the water," Twizzle said to herself.

"But it could be a boat scraping a rock or hitting a log. Maybe I have visitors!"

As Twizzle raced to the beach, scanning the lake for a boat, she smacked into something.

Her heart raced. It was the giant.

She hollered and waved the branch. But the giant didn't budge.

The giant wore Twizzle's hammock on his head like a crown.

Her canoe curled around his waist like a tutu.

Twizzle's garden gate clung to his legs.

And her muddy clothesline trailed behind him like a long, lumpy tail.

As Twizzle stared at her broken belongings, her fear turned into anger.

But when she gazed into the giant's big brown eyes, her anger melted into compassion.

Twizzle slowly inched toward the giant. Something about the bowtie on his dewlap looked familiar. She inched closer still. It wasn't a bowtie after all.

"Hooray!" Twizzle shouted. "You found my favorite fishing lure!"

Twizzle untangled the giant from her canoe, her hammock, her clothesline, her gate, and her fishing lure. Only then could she see he was not a giant in high heels.

He was a moose.

In a flash, the moose scrambled to his feet and ran off.

"Wait," Twizzle called after him.

The moose stopped and turned around.

"I'm Twizzle. What's your name?"

"Zelmor," he answered, as he turned to run away again.

"Please stay, Zelmor," Twizzle pleaded.

"After I destroyed all your stuff?" Zelmor asked.

"It was a bumpy beginning, but we can fix that." Twizzle insisted.

Zelmor didn't say anything. Instead, he began raking a new garden for Twizzle with his antlers.

Zelmor washed the clothes he'd dragged through the dirt and hung them from his antlers to dry.

Zelmor borrowed Twizzle's shirt and tied it across the palm of his antlers.

"Try your new hammock." Zelmor knelt, so Twizzle could climb aboard.

"It's way better than the old one," she cried, as she rocked back and forth.

With Twizzle swinging from his antlers, Zelmor plunged into the lake.

"Hey, what are you doing?" Twizzle shrieked.

"I'm your new canoe. You can fish from my back."

Zelmor sped up, creating a wake behind him. "Tomorrow I'll take you water skiing."

That evening, as the grapefruit moon rose, Twizzle let out a frightful squawk. "How'd you like my moose impersonation?" she asked proudly.

"Uh... keep practicing," Zelmor replied. "It sounded more like a sick goose." They laughed until their bellies hurt.

Fireflies flickered like diamonds in the dark, as Twizzle and Zelmor feasted on fiddlehead ferns and seaweed soup.

Twizzle brushed the thorns from Zelmor's coat and wove wildflowers through his antlers.

Stars popped out like glitter sprinkled on black velvet. Frogs and crickets sang a lullaby that echoed around the lake.

Twizzle leaned against Zelmor. Her eyelids grew heavy. Together, they drifted into dreamland.

The End

# Thank You

To my grandmother and role model, Carol Ryrie Brink, who authored more than 30 books, including the Newbery Award winning *Caddie Woodlawn*.

To my son Will who first entertained the family with tales of a moose named Zelmor.

To my sister Anne who provided encouragement and editing expertise throughout the creation of this book.

To my granddaughter Marion whose nickname, "Twizzle," I borrowed for this story.

To my children, Will, Marguerite, David, and Elizabeth, whom I adore and admire.

To Julia Soplop, author, photographer, and founder of Hill Press, whose patience and guidance helped me navigate the self-publishing process.

To the cottage on Lake Windigo, which helped shape this story and my life story.

Made in the USA
Coppell, TX
14 August 2021